Chicago Bulls

Michael E. Goodman

CREATIVE C EDUCATION

Published by Creative Education
123 South Broad Street, Mankato, Minnesota 56001
Creative Education is an imprint of The Creative Company

Designed by Rita Marshall

Photos by: Allsport Photography, Associated Press/Wide World Photos,
Focus on Sports, NBA Photos, UPI/Corbis-Bettmann, and SportsChrome.

Photo page 1: Michael Jordan
Photo title page: Toni Kukoc

Library of Congress Cataloging-in-Publication Data

Goodman, Michael E.
Chicago Bulls / Michael E. Goodman.
p. cm. — (NBA today)
Summary: Highlights the history and key players and coaches of the
Chicago Bulls.
ISBN 0-88682-869-4

1. Chicago Bulls (Basketball team)—Juvenile literature.
[1. Chicago Bulls (Basketball team)—History. 2. Basketball—History.]
I. Title. II. Series: NBA today (Mankato, Minn.)

GV885.52.C45G66 1997   96-53021
796.323'64'0977311—dc21

First edition

5 4 3 2 1

The American poet Carl Sandburg referred to Chicago as the "City of Big Shoulders," paying homage to both its size and power. Boasting one of the world's tallest buildings, the world's busiest airport, and some of the world's largest stores and commercial buildings, Chicago has earned a well-deserved reputation for bigness. With its factories, rail yards, and stockyards—and the powerful winds buffeting the city from Lake Michigan—Chicago's strength is legendary.

Chicago residents are fiercely proud of their city. They are particularly devoted to its professional sports franchises—the baseball Cubs and White Sox, the football Bears, the

Chicago great Walt Bellamy.

hockey Blackhawks, and the basketball Bulls. While baseball, football, and hockey have nearly always had strong fan support in Chicago, basketball was a late bloomer in the Windy City. In fact, the Bulls are Chicago's fourth pro basketball franchise, and the first one to succeed.

Today's team, behind coach Phil Jackson, is reaching heights to equal the majestic Sears Tower, thanks to the presence of the highest-flying of all NBA stars, Michael Jordan, and his teammate Scottie Pippen. They brought Chicago its first National Basketball Association (NBA) championship in 1991. Now, after several more championships, the Bulls have become the powerhouse of the '90s.

1 9 2 6

George Halas's Bruins won only nine of 30 games in their inaugural ABL season.

THE ROCKY ROAD FROM BRUINS TO BULLS

The story of professional basketball in Chicago begins in 1925 with the formation of the Chicago Bruins as a charter member of the American Basketball League (ABL), the first real pro circuit. The Bruins' owner was George Halas, who also founded and owned the football Bears.

But sports fans were not ready for professional basketball in the 1920s, and few spectators turned out to see the slow-moving games in which teams seldom scored more than 30 points each. The Bruins lasted only six years, folding with the rest of the league in 1931 at the beginning of the Great Depression. Halas made an attempt to revive the Bruins in the early 1940s as part of the new National Basketball League (NBL), but the club quickly went out of business.

In 1946, another NBL team, the Gears, was established in Chicago. To assure the team's success, its owner signed up

The fiery Scottie Pippen.

Max Zaslofsky, a future Hall of Famer, led the Stags in scoring for the fourth straight year.

the most popular college basketball player of the day, George Mikan, a recent graduate of DePaul University in Chicago. With his size and unstoppable hook shot, the 6-foot-10 Mikan was an offensive force unlike any pro player before him.

Mikan led the Gears to the NBL championship during his first season with the club, and Chicago fans believed a sports dynasty was in the making. Then a strange thing happened. The next year, the Gears' owner decided to form a new league with his team at its center. That circuit went broke within a few months, however, and the Chicago players were distributed to various NBL teams. George Mikan ended up with the Minneapolis Lakers, where he did indeed establish pro basketball's first dynasty.

Meanwhile, the Basketball Association of America (BAA) had also launched a franchise in the Windy City. The team, called the Stags, played well enough during its first season, 1946–47, to capture the league's Western Division title.

The Stags continued to perform before small crowds at home for the next few years as a member of the BAA. Eventually they joined the new National Basketball Association (NBA), which was formed when the BAA and NBL merged before the 1949–50 season. But lack of fan interest in Chicago once again led to financial problems, and the Stags folded after only one NBA campaign.

Eleven years passed before the NBA decided to establish another franchise in Chicago. Following a familiar pattern, that club also had problems getting off the ground. Called the Packers because its home court was located near the world-famous Chicago stockyards, the new Chicago team made immediate headlines by drafting the best college player in the country, 6-foot-11 center Walt Bellamy. In Chicago, Bellamy averaged 30.6 points per game, second in the league behind Wilt Chamberlain, and was an easy choice for Rookie of the Year.

Unfortunately, the Packers did not have as fine a rookie season as Bellamy. Despite the big center's strong play, the club won only 18 games and drew very small crowds. Before the 1962–63 season, the team changed its name to the Zephyrs and moved to a smaller arena. But it still had trouble winning games and filling the stands. The next year, the club left Chicago for good to become the Baltimore Bullets.

Luckily for Chicago basketball fans, the leaders of the NBA still believed that the Windy City could support a pro basketball team. So, in 1966, the league tried again, approving a new franchise to be called the Bulls. This Chicago team was here to stay.

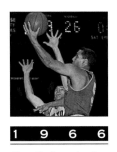

1 9 6 6

Guy Rodgers had a team-record 24 assists in a 110–107 win over the New York Knicks.

KERR AND SLOAN PROVIDE A LOCAL TOUCH

The Bulls' owners wanted to get local fans behind the team right away, so they brought in Chicago native John Kerr as the club's first coach. As a player, Kerr had starred at the University of Illinois. He went on to play more than a decade in the NBA in Syracuse and Philadelphia.

In another good public relations move, the Bulls selected Jerry Sloan as their first pick in the expansion draft. Sloan had grown up in southern Illinois and had led nearby Evansville University to two national small-college championships. He turned out to be more than just a public relations gimmick for

Artis Gilmore starred for Chicago in the late 1970s.

The hustling Bob Weiss was an earlier standout. 11

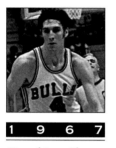

Guard Jerry Sloan and his teammate Guy Rodgers were named to the West All-Star team.

the club; with his strong work ethic and never-say-die attitude on the court, Sloan quickly became the heart and soul of the Bulls and served as the team's leader for the next decade.

Dick Motta, who coached the Bulls after Kerr, marveled at the way Sloan hustled. "Jerry was not physically gifted," said Motta, "but he used to set goals for every game that would help his team win. For instance, he would determine to get eight rebounds, even playing in the backcourt. He would take three charges, come up with three loose balls, and hold his man 10 points under his average. By doing these things, he contributed to his team in many ways."

Even the presence of Kerr and Sloan did not convince Chicago fans that the Bulls were a team worth watching. Only 4,200 fans showed up for the club's first home game on October 18, 1966, against the powerful San Francisco Warriors. But that small crowd was treated to a big surprise. Sloan sizzled, scoring a game-high 26 points, and the Bulls grabbed the victory, 119–116.

As the Bulls' charter season wore on, more and more fans discovered the team. Sloan, his backcourt partner Guy Rodgers, and power forward Bob Boozer led the club in scoring, while Rodgers topped the entire league in assists.

During the stretch drive to the playoffs, the young Bulls came into their own. They won eight of their last 12 games, including a victory over Wilt Chamberlain's 76ers that clinched a postseason berth for Chicago. Although Philadelphia would eventually go on to win the NBA title that year, Chicago received nearly as much publicity by virtue of its reaching the playoffs.

"I don't know anybody who had the success we had that

first year, what with us making the playoffs," said a beaming Johnny Kerr. "No expansion team had ever done that. I was named Coach of the Year. I had so much fun because we took guys who were eighth and ninth players on their old teams and molded them into winners."

Kerr's excitement was short-lived, however. Chicago started out its second season by losing 15 of its first 16 games. One of the reasons for the team's falloff was the decision to trade Guy Rodgers to Cincinnati for Flynn Robinson and several high draft choices. Neither Robinson nor backup guard Clem Haskins had Rodgers's court savvy, and the Bulls wound up last in the league in offense. Still, they did manage to sneak into the playoffs again.

1 9 6 8

The Bulls' leader in rebounds, Jim Washington, was also the team's best defender.

DICK MOTTA DOES THINGS HIS WAY

Before the 1968–69 season, the Bulls' owners decided that a coaching change was needed to improve the club. They turned to a little-known college coach named Dick Motta and offered him the job. Motta had followed an unusual path to reach the NBA. He hadn't played college or pro basketball and, in fact, had been cut from his high school team. It would be a challenge, but he jumped at the chance to direct the Bulls.

"Things were in the pits in Chicago when I first got there," Motta recalled. "The club had only 38 season-ticket holders at the time."

Things weren't much better on the court. The Bulls didn't have a great offense, and their defense—the part of the game that meant the most to Motta—was terrible. Motta felt the

All-Star Bob Boozer led the Bulls in scoring with a 21.7 average.

biggest culprit was guard Flynn Robinson, a good shooter who seldom guarded his man. Motta and Robinson clashed, and the coach decided to show who was boss right away. He told team owners, "If Flynn Robinson is here when I come to practice tomorrow morning, get yourself a new coach." Robinson was quickly traded to Milwaukee for two reserve players, forward Bob Love and guard Bob Weiss. Both acquisitions played key roles in the Bulls' revival under Motta.

Other players who Motta brought to Chicago included centers Tom Boerwinkle and Walt Wesley and All-Star forward Chet "the Jet" Walker. All were hard-nosed competitors who met Motta's requirements for hustle and tight defensive play. But the player who most characterized Motta's system was Jerry Sloan, who was named to the NBA's All-Defensive team six times in his 10-year Chicago career.

Behind Motta's coaching and the tough play of their team leaders, the Bulls began a steady rise in the NBA standings. They went from fifth place in their division during Motta's first season, 1968–69, to first place in 1974–75. The coach's strategy was to grind the opposition's offense to a halt with a smothering defense. Three times during Motta's seven-year reign, Chicago led the NBA in fewest points allowed. With Motta riding officials and his own players, and with Jerry Sloan and teammates fighting for loose balls, there was seldom a dull moment during a Bulls game. Chicago fans loved watching their heroes play, even in losses, and opposing teams hated facing the Bulls.

During the 1970–71 season, the Bulls achieved their first winning record, an impressive 51–31 mark, and Motta was named Coach of the Year. The next year the team's record

The reliable Bob Love.

improved to 57–25, thanks in large part to the addition of point guard Norm Van Lier. What Van Lier brought to the Bulls was blazing speed, all-out defense, and a keen ability to spot the open man.

Coach Motta now had all of the components in place to make a run for the NBA title. Sloan and Van Lier formed an incomparable backcourt, while Chet Walker and Bob Love handled the bulk of the team's scoring. Walker was a bruiser underneath the basket, and Love developed a technique for slipping away from his man for easy hoops. Boerwinkle and Clifford Ray shared the center spot and much of the rebounding work; they also set some of the hardest screens in the game. Bob Weiss came off the bench as the club's sixth man and provided quick offense and solid defense. Said basketball executive Stu Inman, "I think when the history of the NBA is written, we'll find that team advanced the technical aspects of basketball to a great extent."

1 9 7 0

Using his bulk to get position, center Tom Boerwinkle logged the Chicago Bulls' first 1,000-rebound season.

PLAYOFF FAILURES AND SUCCESSES

Motta's crew compiled outstanding records during the regular season, but didn't perform as well in the playoffs. Chicago was eliminated in the first round every year until the 1973–74 campaign. The club conquered the Detroit Pistons in a tight seven-game battle for its first playoff-series triumph. But the team's balloon quickly burst this time, too: The Bulls were wiped out in the conference finals, four games to none, by Kareem Abdul-Jabbar and the Bucks.

"We were extremely demoralized by the sweep," recalled Jerry Sloan, "but we knew we could bounce back. We had a

16

tough-guy image of ourselves. All we could think about was coming back the next year and getting revenge."

Despite this determination, the Bulls had a slow start the next season. Walker was a step slower and Boerwinkle was bothered by sore knees. Van Lier and Love both threatened to leave Chicago over salary disputes. But then the Bulls made a key move, sending Clifford Ray to Golden State for All-Star center Nate Thurmond. In the season opener, Thurmond blocked a team-record 12 shots to lead the Bulls to a 120–115 victory over Atlanta.

That year, Thurmond's intense play and leadership helped the Bulls capture their first division title and move on to the conference finals against the Golden State Warriors.

But the Bulls lost the series, and when Chet Walker and Jerry Sloan retired, and Nate Thurmond was traded away, the Bulls' record sank to 24–58 in 1975–76. When coach Motta was fired, fans wondered what would happen next.

Bob Love's scoring average of 25.8 helped him earn All-NBA honors.

Big bad Artis Gilmore comes to town

The fans got their answer quickly. The team began to rebuild immediately when it drafted Artis Gilmore from a pool of players made available after the American Basketball Association (ABA) went out of business in 1976. The 7-foot-2 Gilmore had been one of the ABA's top stars with the Kentucky Colonels. With his huge size and defensive intensity on the court, Gilmore was the type of player that Chicago fans admired the most. "Aside from Wilt Chamberlain, Artis Gilmore is the strongest man ever to play this game," said veteran NBA coach Hubie Brown.

Dick Motta's squads displayed great teamwork (pages 18–19).

Norm Van Lier was named to the West All-Star team and the NBA's All-Defensive first team.

Teamed with Mickey Johnson and rookie Scott May up front, and supported by Norm Van Lier and Wilbur Holland in the backcourt, Gilmore helped guide the Bulls back into the playoffs with a 44–38 record. He averaged 18 points per game, blocked more than 200 shots, and ranked fourth in the league in rebounding.

But even big Artis Gilmore could not push the Bulls past Bill Walton and the Portland Trail Blazers in the playoffs. The Blazers took the opening-round series, two games to one, on their way to the NBA championship.

Gilmore continued to lead Chicago on both offense and defense during the next two seasons and was joined the second year by high-scoring rookie guard Reggie Theus. But injuries hampered several other key players, and the club failed to make the playoffs either year. Then, in an effort to rekindle some of the team's old magic, Jerry Sloan was brought in as coach in 1979–80.

As a player, Sloan had given the Bulls all-out intensity, and he expected the same from the men he coached. "If there's a loose ball and nobody goes for it, I don't care if the score is 100–50, I'm going to come down on somebody hard," Sloan promised fans.

Over the next two seasons, Sloan assembled one of the biggest and most intimidating lineups in the NBA. The backcourt consisted of 6-foot-8 Reggie Theus and 6-foot-7 Bob Wilkerson. Up front were forwards Larry Kenon and David Greenwood, each 6-foot-9, and giant center Artis Gilmore. This group won 45 games during 1980–81 and reached the second round of the playoffs. Sportswriters voted the Bulls the NBA's Most Improved Club.

It is difficult to describe what happened next. During the following season, the Bulls turned quickly from winners to also-rans. A writer for the *NBA Guide* blamed Chicago's disappointing tumble from second to fifth place in the Central Division in 1981–82 on "strange chemistry." Other reasons for the falloff were poor defense and an inability to win away from Chicago Stadium. At any rate, when the team won only 19 of its first 51 games, Jerry Sloan was fired and general manager Rod Thorn finished the year as interim coach. Thorn was followed by Paul Westhead and Kevin Loughery during the next two seasons, but neither could put together a winning combination.

Then came September 12, 1984—perhaps the most significant day in the history of the Bulls. That was the day Chicago owners announced the signing of their top draft pick, Michael Jordan, to a contract. The franchise and the league would never be quite the same.

1 9 8 0

The Bulls' David Greenwood joined NBA superstars Larry Bird and Magic Johnson on the All-Rookie team.

"AIR" JORDAN STARTS THE BULLS SOARING

The NBA had featured other great leapers before Michael Jordan, and other great long-range shooters, dunk-shot artists, and quick-handed ball thieves. But it had never seen all of those talents wrapped up in one player. Jordan was a complete package, and Chicago fans quickly fell in love with Jordan's skills and personality. Average attendance in Chicago Stadium nearly doubled from 6,365 to 11,887 during Jordan's rookie campaign. The media nicknamed him "Air" because of his ability to soar skyward and float toward the basket as if he were on a spacewalk.

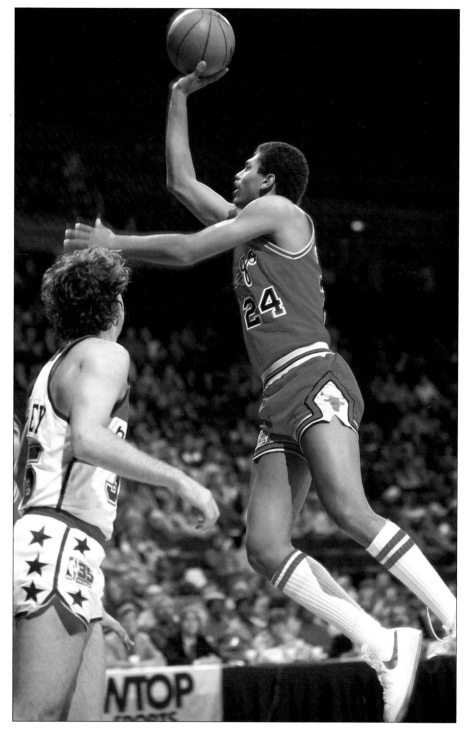

The explosive Reggie Theus.

Jordan earned the respect of local fans not only for his remarkable natural ability, but also for his work ethic. One of his most embarrassing moments had come several years before when he was cut from his high school team. "After that, whenever I worked out, got tired, and figured I should stop, I'd close my eyes and see that list without my name on it," Jordan remembered. "That usually got me going again."

1 9 8 2

All-Star Artis Gilmore led the Bulls in scoring, rebounding, shooting, and shot-blocking.

The Bulls' fortunes began rising as soon as Jordan joined the team. During his first season in Chicago, he led the club back to the playoffs for the first time in four years with a 38–44 record. The Bulls have earned a berth in the postseason tournament every year since. And even as he piled up individual honors—including NBA Rookie of the Year, league MVP, scoring champion, first-team All-NBA, Defensive Player of the Year, and NBA All-Defensive team (many of them several times)—Jordan has never lost sight of his role as a team player. That is something that cannot be said about many of the great scorers in NBA history.

During Jordan's first two years in Chicago, many fans viewed him as a one-man team. Other Bulls players—Orlando Woolridge, Charles Oakley, John Paxson, Dave Corzine, and Brad Sellers—were solid but unspectacular. It was Jordan who made the lineup dangerous.

Then, during the 1987–88 college draft, Chicago management picked up two outstanding players: 6-foot-8 swingman Scottie Pippen, out of tiny Central Arkansas, and 6-foot-10 power forward Horace Grant from Clemson. Both struggled at first, but then came into their own. In fact, by the early 1990s, Pippen, labeled by *Basketball Digest* as "the NBA's newest superstar," had helped change the Chicago Bulls into a multithreat team.

1 9 8 7

Forward Charles Oakley ranked second in the NBA with 1,074 rebounds.

STEP-BY-STEP TO A CHAMPIONSHIP

With Jordan at the top of his game and new components added to the Bulls machine, Chicago fans began to believe their club had championship potential. The 1987–88 club made it to the second round of the playoffs. The 1988–89 team went one round further, thanks in part to the addition of center Bill Cartwright, obtained in a trade with the New York Knicks, and the direction of new head coach Phil Jackson.

The 1988–89 playoffs featured one of the most exciting endings in NBA history. In the closing seconds of the final game of a first-round battle between the Bulls and the Cleveland Cavaliers, Cavs guard Craig Ehlo hit a driving layup, and it appeared to be over for Chicago. But with only four seconds left, Jordan took the inbounds pass, faked right, moved left, and lofted a 15-foot "buzzer beater" through the hoop for a one-point Chicago win.

Chicago fans hoped the momentum gained from that miracle shot would propel the Bulls all the way to the finals, but it was not to be. For the second straight year, Chicago fell to its archrival, the Detroit Pistons, and was eliminated from the playoffs. In 1989–90, when the same thing happened a third time, frustrated Bulls supporters began to wonder if their club would ever get past Detroit.

By the next season, however, the Pistons were starting to age, while such Bulls as Pippen, Grant, and young guard B.J.

Armstrong were just beginning to hit their stride. Chicago also had outstanding veteran support in Cartwright and Paxson. With Jordan and Pippen directing the offense and sharing much of the glory, the Bulls finally climbed past the Pistons in the regular-season standings, winning the Central Division title by a full 11 games. Then, to make their revenge complete, the Bulls swept Detroit in the Eastern Conference finals to reach the championship round for the first time in club history. Chicago didn't stop there, either. It took only five games for the Bulls to eliminate the Los Angeles Lakers and bring an NBA crown to the Windy City.

1 9 9 0

Phil Jackson's Bulls set team records for consecutive wins at home (15) and on the road (8).

THE POWERHOUSE OF THE '90S

That first championship was only the beginning. In 1991–92, Jordan's and Pippen's inspired play resulted in a 67–15 record—the best yet in franchise history. The Bulls made it to the finals again, surprising no one. In game six of the championship series, against a tough Portland team, Chicago held a 3–2 advantage. Entering the fourth quarter, Chicago trailed by 15 points. They responded with a 14–2 run; it was the biggest fourth-quarter comeback in finals history. The Bulls had become only the second NBA team to win back-to-back titles.

In 1992–93, the Bulls never lost more than two games in a row. Jordan was on a mission. In the Eastern Conference finals, the Bulls beat coach Pat Riley and the New York Knicks. Many experts had predicted that New York—with its dominating center, Patrick Ewing—would win it all. The Bulls proved the experts wrong. Then they faced Charles

A living legend, Michael Jordan (pages 26–27).

Guard B. J. Armstrong's .435 three-point field goal percentage was the best in the NBA.

Barkley and the Phoenix Suns in the championship series. In game six, Bulls guard John Paxson nailed a three-pointer with only seconds to go, giving Chicago a 99–98 victory. The Bulls became the first team in 27 seasons to win three consecutive championships.

Then, at age 30, Jordan decided he had done all he could do in the NBA. He stunned the sports world when he announced his retirement. He left basketball to give professional baseball a try. The man who was possibly the greatest player in NBA history—whose moves on the court were compared to both poetry and jazz—had called it quits, and nobody knew if the game would ever be the same again.

Pippen became the Bulls' leader, and though they failed to win a fourth championship in row, they added a player who they hoped would get them there—Toni Kukoc. The 6-foot-11 native of Croatia was hailed as a tall man with a sweet scoring touch. He had been the European Player of the Year three times and had won three European championships. Kukoc gave the Bulls hope for the future, especially after Horace Grant left and signed with Orlando.

In 1995–96, the Pippen-led Bulls moved into a new home, the United Center. Pippen showcased his all-around talents and was named to the All-NBA first team. Kukoc became a starter, averaging 15.7 points per game. But the Bulls merely hovered around the .500 mark through most of the season. Then came March 18, when Michael Jordan again stunned the world, announcing, "I'm back." But Jordan's return wasn't enough to lift the Bulls into the finals. It did, however, give them optimism for the future.

Jordan had become less of a scorer and more of a team

player. In 1995–96, with the addition of the flamboyant Dennis Rodman—one the NBA's all-time top rebounders—Chicago evolved into what many people were calling the greatest team ever. Their 72–10 regular-season record was the best the NBA had ever seen, and much of the improvement was due to Rodman's play under the boards. Rodman was an experienced player—he had won two championships in Detroit, had been named the NBA Defensive Player of the Year twice, and was the runner-up two other times.

1 9 9 6

Dennis Rodman captured his fifth straight NBA rebounding title with a 14.9 average.

The Bulls surged through the playoffs, losing only one game before the finals. They then eliminated Seattle in six games, and became, on paper, the best team in NBA history. "This has been a very, very special year," said a smiling Jordan. "There's no way we can really describe it. There was no animosity. There was no bickering. There was no jealousy. This team is very amazing."

In 1996–97, the Bulls battled injuries to Kukoc and Rodman. Taking up the slack were point guard Ron Harper, sharpshooter Steve Kerr, Australian center Luc Longley, and center Brian Williams, a midseason acquisition. The Bulls ended the regular season with a 69–13 record. But when they entered the playoffs, many thought the Bulls were playing lackluster ball. Jordan, however, seemed to have a switch that he could turn on whenever the team needed him to dominate a game. The Bulls plowed through Washington 3–0, Atlanta 4–1, and then Miami 4–1.

Chicago faced the Utah Jazz in the finals. Led by John Stockton and the league's MVP Karl Malone, Utah was coming off its best season ever. The Bulls jumped out to a 2–0 advantage. Game three was played in Utah, where the Jazz

The talented Luc Longley.

Toni Kukoc, a tough competitor.

Robert "the Chief" Parish played in his 21st NBA season, the most in basketball history.

had been virtually unstoppable. Malone and Stockton led Utah to victories in games three and four.

Then, in game five, Jordan was mysteriously absent from the Bulls' pre-game shoot-around. Word spread: Michael Jordan was ill, possibly with the flu or a stomach infection. It was a condition that would have kept most people on the bench or in bed. But Jordon rallied to score 38 points and lead the Bulls to victory.

Jordan proved his selflessness in game six. With less than a minute remaining, he dished off to an open Steve Kerr who sank the go-ahead basket from the top of the key. The Bulls were again world champions, having won the title for the fifth time in seven years.

There is no reason to doubt that as long as the Bulls stay together, their dominance will continue, and Chicago, a city that at one time couldn't keep a franchise, will enjoy watching what many believe is the best team ever.